HOW TO USE THIS JOURNAL

This journal was created as a tool to aid in your devotional time with God. Use the bullet point page for organization made simple. There you can plan your day, set goals and add prayer requests. The guided journal pages allow you to dive deep in the word, starting and ending your day with God. Remember, prayer is a dialogue between you and God. As you pray use the final page to note what He speaks to you.

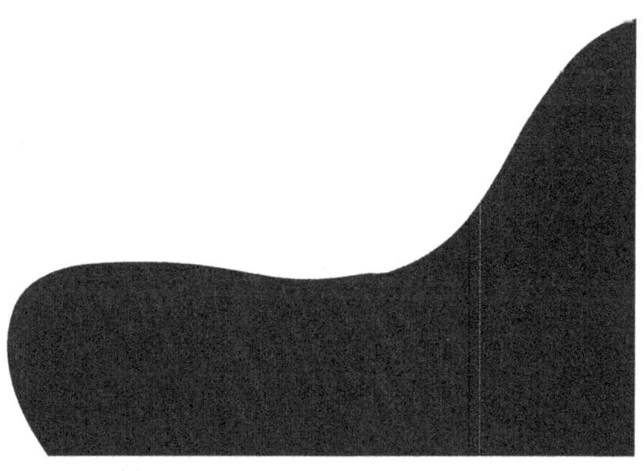

Hey girl,

GOD DESIRES FOR US TO HAVE A HEART THAT IS COMPLETELY SURRENDERED TO HIM. THERE IS NO BETTER TIME THAN NOW TO GIVE HIM A FRESH YES! I ENCOURAGE YOU TO ALLOW GOD TO HAVE HIS WAY IN EVERY AREA OF YOUR LIFE.

I PRAY THAT YOU FIND THIS JOURNAL USEFUL AS YOU WALK WITH GOD. GROWING INTO THE GODLY WOMAN HE CALLED YOU TO BE, LOVING OTHERS AND YOURSELF WITH THE LOVE OF CHRIST, AND BEING MOTIVATED TO PURSUE YOUR GOALS.

love, Jorey Bell

date: ____________

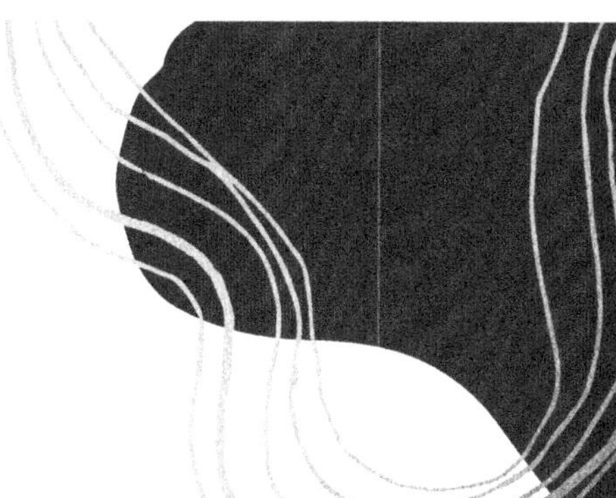

GOALS

♡ ____________________

♡ ____________________

♡ ____________________

TO-DOS

♡ ____________________

♡ ____________________

♡ ____________________

PRAYER POINTS

♡ ____________________

♡ ____________________

♡ ____________________

And the LORD, He is the One who goes before you. He will be with you,
He will not leave you nor forsake you; do not fear nor be dismayed.
Deuteronomy 31:8 NKJV

But seek first the kingdom of God and His righteousness,
and all these things shall be added to you.
Matthew 6:33 NKJV

Evening

I will both lie down in peace, and sleep;
For You alone, O Lord, make me dwell in safety.
Palms 4:8 NKJV

WHAT IS GOD SAYING?

Then you will call upon Me and go and pray to Me, and I will listen to you.
Jeremiah 29:12 NKJV

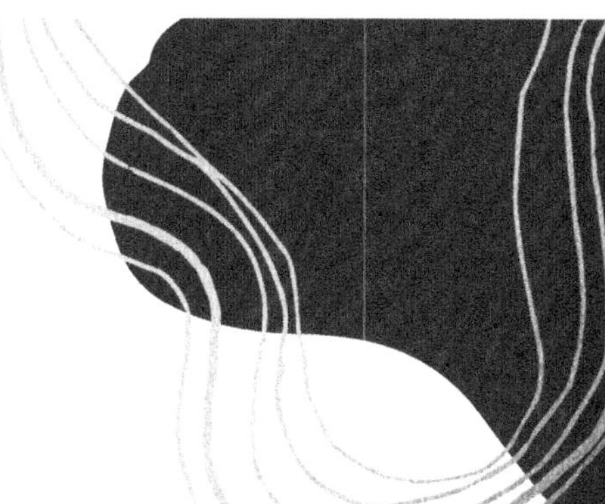

date:___________

GOALS

♡ ____________________

♡ ____________________

♡ ____________________

TO-DOS

♡ ____________________

♡ ____________________

♡ ____________________

PRAYER POINTS

♡ ____________________

♡ ____________________

♡ ____________________

And the LORD, He is the One who goes before you. He will be with you,
He will not leave you nor forsake you; do not fear nor be dismayed.
Deuteronomy 31:8 NKJV

But seek first the kingdom of God and His righteousness,
and all these things shall be added to you.
Matthew 6:33 NKJV

Evening

I will both lie down in peace, and sleep;
For You alone, O Lord, make me dwell in safety.
Palms 4:8 NKJV

WHAT IS GOD SAYING?

Then you will call upon Me and go and pray to Me, and I will listen to you.
Jeremiah 29:12 NKJV

date: ____________

GOALS

♡ ______________________________
♡ ______________________________
♡ ______________________________

TO-DOS

♡ ______________________________
♡ ______________________________
♡ ______________________________

PRAYER POINTS

♡ ______________________________
♡ ______________________________
♡ ______________________________

And the LORD, He is the One who goes before you. He will be with you,
He will not leave you nor forsake you; do not fear nor be dismayed.
Deuteronomy 31:8 NKJV

But seek first the kingdom of God and His righteousness,
and all these things shall be added to you.
Matthew 6:33 NKJV

Evening

I will both lie down in peace, and sleep;
For You alone, O Lord, make me dwell in safety.
Palms 4:8 NKJV

WHAT IS GOD SAYING?

Then you will call upon Me and go and pray to Me, and I will listen to you.
Jeremiah 29:12 NKJV

date:

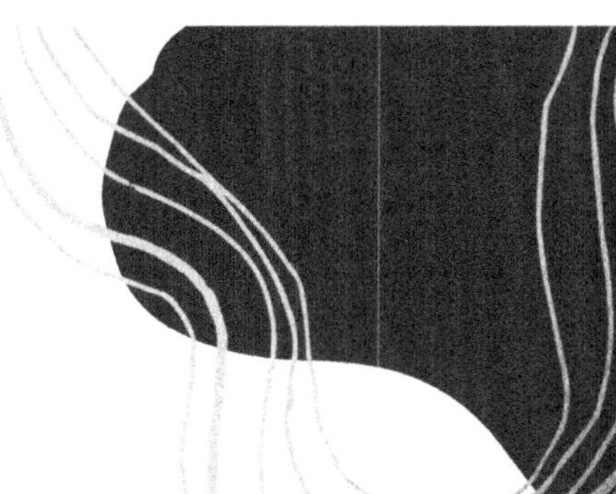

GOALS

♡

♡

♡

TO-DOS

♡

♡

♡

PRAYER POINTS

♡

♡

♡

And the LORD, He is the One who goes before you. He will be with you, He will not leave you nor forsake you; do not fear nor be dismayed.
Deuteronomy 31:8 NKJV

But seek first the kingdom of God and His righteousness,
and all these things shall be added to you.
Matthew 6:33 NKJV

Evening

I will both lie down in peace, and sleep;
For You alone, O Lord, make me dwell in safety.
Palms 4:8 NKJV

WHAT IS GOD SAYING?

Then you will call upon Me and go and pray to Me, and I will listen to you.
Jeremiah 29:12 NKJV

date: ____________

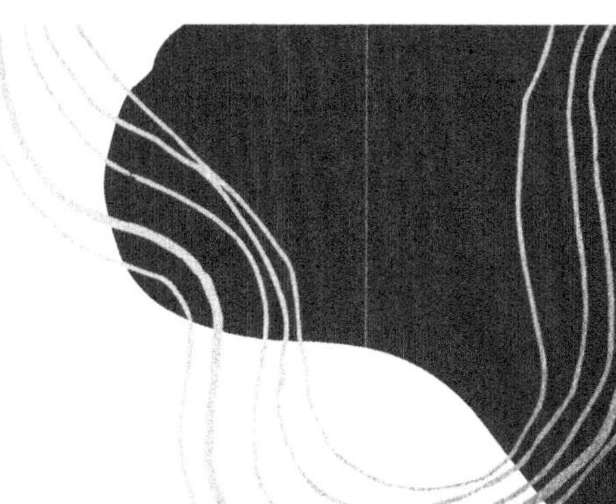

GOALS

♡ ______________________________

♡ ______________________________

♡ ______________________________

TO-DOS

♡ ______________________________

♡ ______________________________

♡ ______________________________

PRAYER POINTS

♡ ______________________________

♡ ______________________________

♡ ______________________________

And the LORD, He is the One who goes before you. He will be with you,
He will not leave you nor forsake you; do not fear nor be dismayed.
Deuteronomy 31:8 NKJV

But seek first the kingdom of God and His righteousness,
and all these things shall be added to you.
Matthew 6:33 NKJV

Evening

I will both lie down in peace, and sleep;
For You alone, O Lord, make me dwell in safety.
Palms 4:8 NKJV

WHAT IS GOD SAYING?

Then you will call upon Me and go and pray to Me, and I will listen to you.
Jeremiah 29:12 NKJV

GOALS

♡ ____

♡ ____

♡ ____

TO-DOS

♡ ____

♡ ____

♡ ____

PRAYER POINTS

♡ ____

♡ ____

♡ ____

And the LORD, He is the One who goes before you. He will be with you, He will not leave you nor forsake you; do not fear nor be dismayed.
Deuteronomy 31:8 NKJV

But seek first the kingdom of God and His righteousness,
and all these things shall be added to you.
Matthew 6:33 NKJV

Evening

I will both lie down in peace, and sleep;
For You alone, O Lord, make me dwell in safety.
Palms 4:8 NKJV

WHAT IS GOD SAYING?

Then you will call upon Me and go and pray to Me, and I will listen to you.
Jeremiah 29:12 NKJV

date: __________

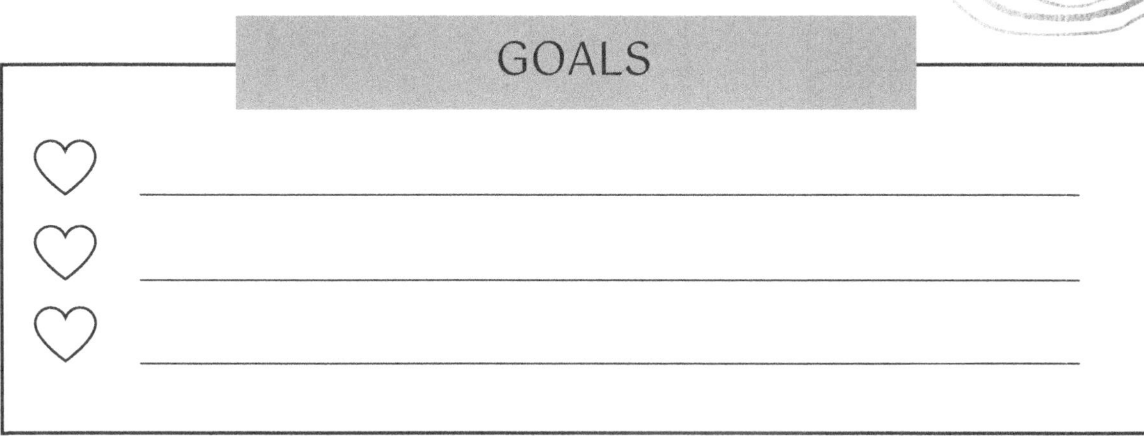

GOALS

TO-DOS

PRAYER POINTS

And the LORD, He is the One who goes before you. He will be with you,
He will not leave you nor forsake you; do not fear nor be dismayed.
Deuteronomy 31:8 NKJV

But seek first the kingdom of God and His righteousness,
and all these things shall be added to you.
Matthew 6:33 NKJV

Evening

I will both lie down in peace, and sleep;
For You alone, O Lord, make me dwell in safety.
Palms 4:8 NKJV

WHAT IS GOD SAYING?

Then you will call upon Me and go and pray to Me, and I will listen to you.
Jeremiah 29:12 NKJV

date:________

GOALS

♡ ____
♡ ____
♡ ____

TO-DOS

♡ ____
♡ ____
♡ ____

PRAYER POINTS

♡ ____
♡ ____
♡ ____

And the LORD, He is the One who goes before you. He will be with you,
He will not leave you nor forsake you; do not fear nor be dismayed.
Deuteronomy 31:8 NKJV

But seek first the kingdom of God and His righteousness,
and all these things shall be added to you.
Matthew 6:33 NKJV

Evening

I will both lie down in peace, and sleep;
For You alone, O Lord, make me dwell in safety.
Palms 4:8 NKJV

WHAT IS GOD SAYING?

Then you will call upon Me and go and pray to Me, and I will listen to you.
Jeremiah 29:12 NKJV

date:________

GOALS

♡ ________

♡ ________

♡ ________

TO-DOS

♡ ________

♡ ________

♡ ________

PRAYER POINTS

♡ ________

♡ ________

♡ ________

And the LORD, He is the One who goes before you. He will be with you,
He will not leave you nor forsake you; do not fear nor be dismayed.
Deuteronomy 31:8 NKJV

But seek first the kingdom of God and His righteousness,
and all these things shall be added to you.
Matthew 6:33 NKJV

Evening

I will both lie down in peace, and sleep;
For You alone, O Lord, make me dwell in safety.
Palms 4:8 NKJV

WHAT IS GOD SAYING?

Then you will call upon Me and go and pray to Me, and I will listen to you.
Jeremiah 29:12 NKJV

date: ________

GOALS

♡ ________

♡ ________

♡ ________

TO-DOS

♡ ________

♡ ________

♡ ________

PRAYER POINTS

♡ ________

♡ ________

♡ ________

And the LORD, He is the One who goes before you. He will be with you,
He will not leave you nor forsake you; do not fear nor be dismayed.
Deuteronomy 31:8 NKJV

But seek first the kingdom of God and His righteousness,
and all these things shall be added to you.
Matthew 6:33 NKJV

Evening

I will both lie down in peace, and sleep;
For You alone, O Lord, make me dwell in safety.
Palms 4:8 NKJV

WHAT IS GOD SAYING?

Then you will call upon Me and go and pray to Me, and I will listen to you.
Jeremiah 29:12 NKJV

date: ______________

GOALS

♡ ______________________

♡ ______________________

♡ ______________________

TO-DOS

♡ ______________________

♡ ______________________

♡ ______________________

PRAYER POINTS

♡ ______________________

♡ ______________________

♡ ______________________

And the LORD, He is the One who goes before you. He will be with you,
He will not leave you nor forsake you; do not fear nor be dismayed.
Deuteronomy 31:8 NKJV

But seek first the kingdom of God and His righteousness,
and all these things shall be added to you.
Matthew 6:33 NKJV

Evening

I will both lie down in peace, and sleep;
For You alone, O Lord, make me dwell in safety.
Palms 4:8 NKJV

WHAT IS GOD SAYING?

Then you will call upon Me and go and pray to Me, and I will listen to you.
Jeremiah 29:12 NKJV

date:

GOALS

TO-DOS

PRAYER POINTS

And the LORD, He is the One who goes before you. He will be with you, He will not leave you nor forsake you; do not fear nor be dismayed.
Deuteronomy 31:8 NKJV

But seek first the kingdom of God and His righteousness,
and all these things shall be added to you.
Matthew 6:33 NKJV

Evening

I will both lie down in peace, and sleep;
For You alone, O Lord, make me dwell in safety.
Palms 4:8 NKJV

WHAT IS GOD SAYING?

Then you will call upon Me and go and pray to Me, and I will listen to you.
Jeremiah 29:12 NKJV

date:

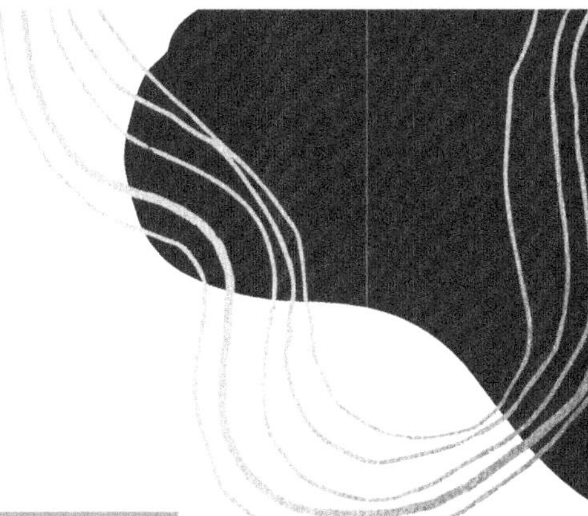

GOALS

♡ ____________________
♡ ____________________
♡ ____________________

TO-DOS

♡ ____________________
♡ ____________________
♡ ____________________

PRAYER POINTS

♡ ____________________
♡ ____________________
♡ ____________________

And the LORD, He is the One who goes before you. He will be with you,
He will not leave you nor forsake you; do not fear nor be dismayed.
Deuteronomy 31:8 NKJV

But seek first the kingdom of God and His righteousness,
and all these things shall be added to you.
Matthew 6:33 NKJV

Evening

I will both lie down in peace, and sleep;
For You alone, O Lord, make me dwell in safety.
Palms 4:8 NKJV

WHAT IS GOD SAYING?

Then you will call upon Me and go and pray to Me, and I will listen to you.
Jeremiah 29:12 NKJV

date: ____________

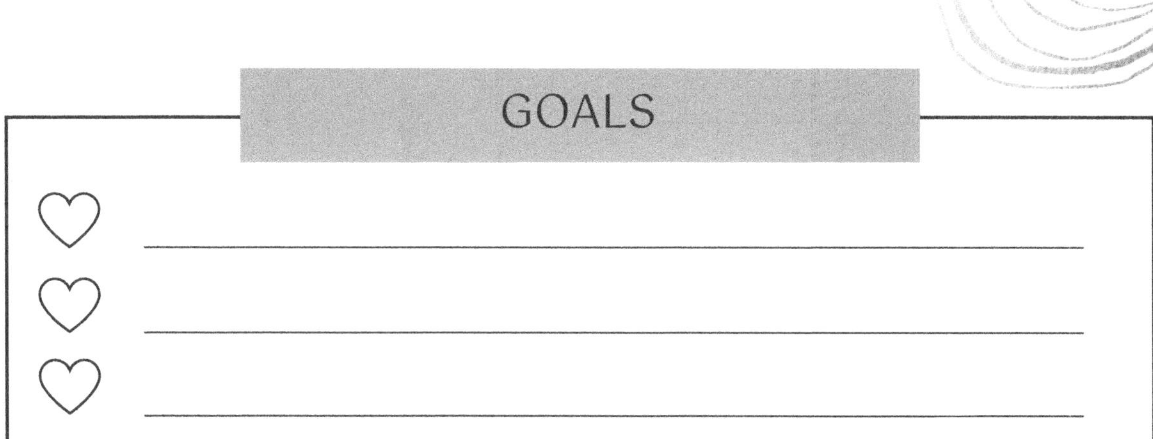

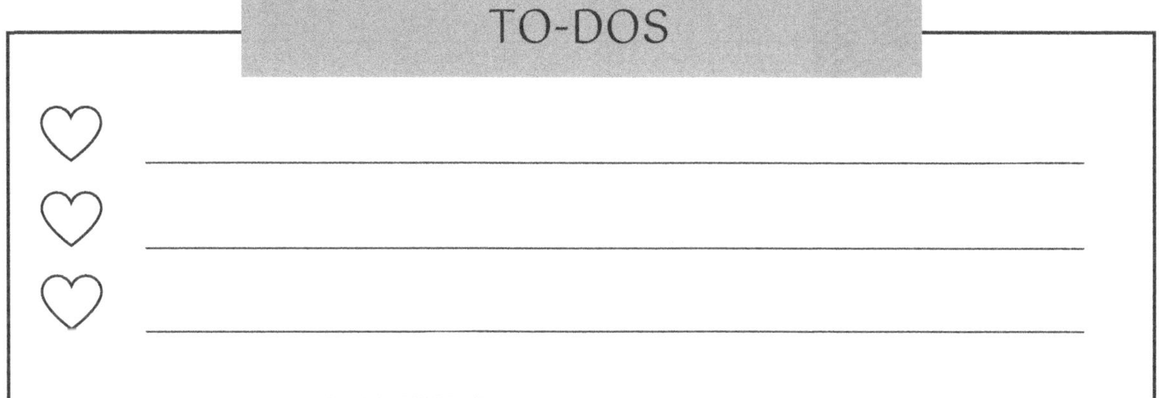

PRAYER POINTS

And the LORD, He is the One who goes before you. He will be with you, He will not leave you nor forsake you; do not fear nor be dismayed.

Deuteronomy 31:8 NKJV

But seek first the kingdom of God and His righteousness,
and all these things shall be added to you.
Matthew 6:33 NKJV

Evening

I will both lie down in peace, and sleep;
For You alone, O Lord, make me dwell in safety.
Palms 4:8 NKJV

WHAT IS GOD SAYING?

Then you will call upon Me and go and pray to Me, and I will listen to you.
Jeremiah 29:12 NKJV

date: ____________

GOALS

♡ ______
♡ ______
♡ ______

TO-DOS

♡ ______
♡ ______
♡ ______

PRAYER POINTS

♡ ______
♡ ______
♡ ______

And the LORD, He is the One who goes before you. He will be with you, He will not leave you nor forsake you; do not fear nor be dismayed.
Deuteronomy 31:8 NKJV

But seek first the kingdom of God and His righteousness,
and all these things shall be added to you.
Matthew 6:33 NKJV

Evening

I will both lie down in peace, and sleep;
For You alone, O Lord, make me dwell in safety.
Palms 4:8 NKJV

WHAT IS GOD SAYING?

Then you will call upon Me and go and pray to Me, and I will listen to you.
Jeremiah 29:12 NKJV

date:

GOALS

♡

♡

♡

TO-DOS

♡

♡

♡

PRAYER POINTS

♡

♡

♡

And the LORD, He is the One who goes before you. He will be with you,
He will not leave you nor forsake you; do not fear nor be dismayed.
Deuteronomy 31:8 NKJV

But seek first the kingdom of God and His righteousness,
and all these things shall be added to you.
Matthew 6:33 NKJV

Evening

I will both lie down in peace, and sleep;
For You alone, O Lord, make me dwell in safety.
Palms 4:8 NKJV

WHAT IS GOD SAYING?

Then you will call upon Me and go and pray to Me, and I will listen to you.
Jeremiah 29:12 NKJV

date: ____________

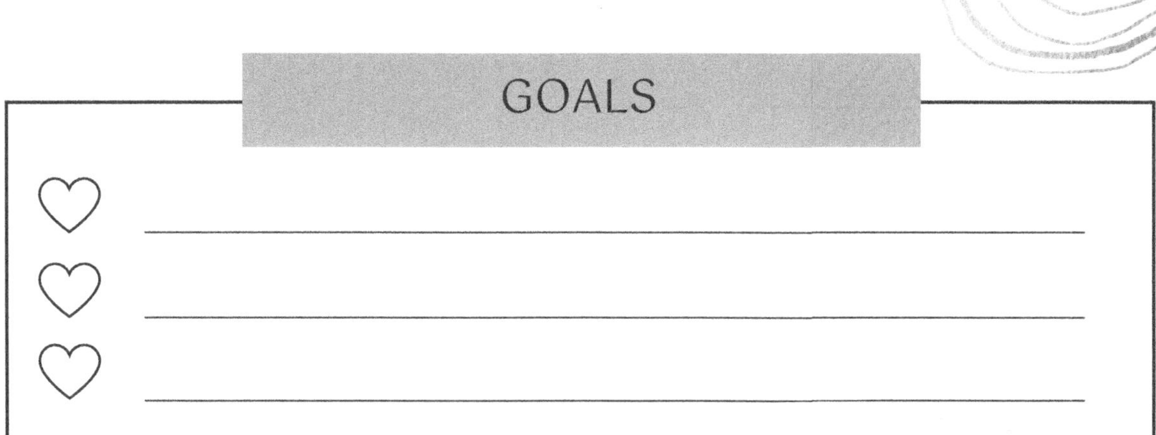

TO-DOS

♡ ____________

♡ ____________

♡ ____________

PRAYER POINTS

♡ ____________

♡ ____________

♡ ____________

And the LORD, He is the One who goes before you. He will be with you, He will not leave you nor forsake you; do not fear nor be dismayed.
Deuteronomy 31:8 NKJV

But seek first the kingdom of God and His righteousness,
and all these things shall be added to you.
Matthew 6:33 NKJV

I will both lie down in peace, and sleep;
For You alone, O Lord, make me dwell in safety.
Palms 4:8 NKJV

WHAT IS GOD SAYING?

Then you will call upon Me and go and pray to Me, and I will listen to you.
Jeremiah 29:12 NKJV

date: ____________

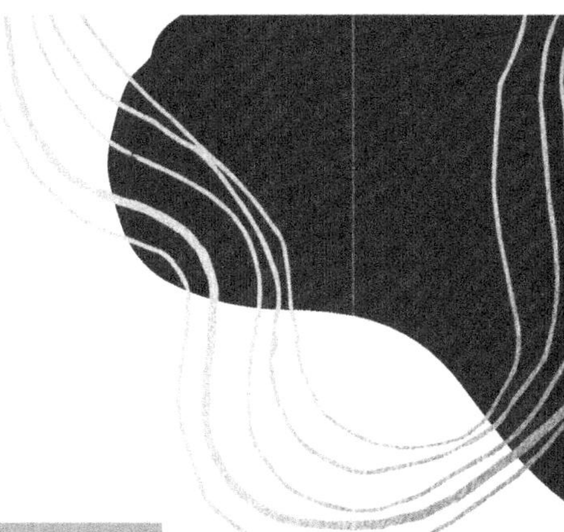

GOALS

♡ ______________________________

♡ ______________________________

♡ ______________________________

TO-DOS

♡ ______________________________

♡ ______________________________

♡ ______________________________

PRAYER POINTS

♡ ______________________________

♡ ______________________________

♡ ______________________________

And the LORD, He is the One who goes before you. He will be with you,
He will not leave you nor forsake you; do not fear nor be dismayed.
Deuteronomy 31:8 NKJV

But seek first the kingdom of God and His righteousness,
and all these things shall be added to you.
Matthew 6:33 NKJV

Evening

I will both lie down in peace, and sleep;
For You alone, O Lord, make me dwell in safety.
Palms 4:8 NKJV

WHAT IS GOD SAYING?

Then you will call upon Me and go and pray to Me, and I will listen to you.
Jeremiah 29:12 NKJV

date: ____________

GOALS

♡ ____________

♡ ____________

♡ ____________

TO-DOS

♡ ____________

♡ ____________

♡ ____________

PRAYER POINTS

♡ ____________

♡ ____________

♡ ____________

And the LORD, He is the One who goes before you. He will be with you,
He will not leave you nor forsake you; do not fear nor be dismayed.
Deuteronomy 31:8 NKJV

But seek first the kingdom of God and His righteousness,
and all these things shall be added to you.
Matthew 6:33 NKJV

Evening

I will both lie down in peace, and sleep;
For You alone, O Lord, make me dwell in safety.
Palms 4:8 NKJV

WHAT IS GOD SAYING?

Then you will call upon Me and go and pray to Me, and I will listen to you.
Jeremiah 29:12 NKJV

date: ______

GOALS

♡ ______

♡ ______

♡ ______

TO-DOS

♡ ______

♡ ______

♡ ______

PRAYER POINTS

♡ ______

♡ ______

♡ ______

And the LORD, He is the One who goes before you. He will be with you, He will not leave you nor forsake you; do not fear nor be dismayed.

Deuteronomy 31:8 NKJV

But seek first the kingdom of God and His righteousness,
and all these things shall be added to you.
Matthew 6:33 NKJV

I will both lie down in peace, and sleep;
For You alone, O Lord, make me dwell in safety.
Palms 4:8 NKJV

WHAT IS GOD SAYING?

Then you will call upon Me and go and pray to Me, and I will listen to you.
Jeremiah 29:12 NKJV

date:__________

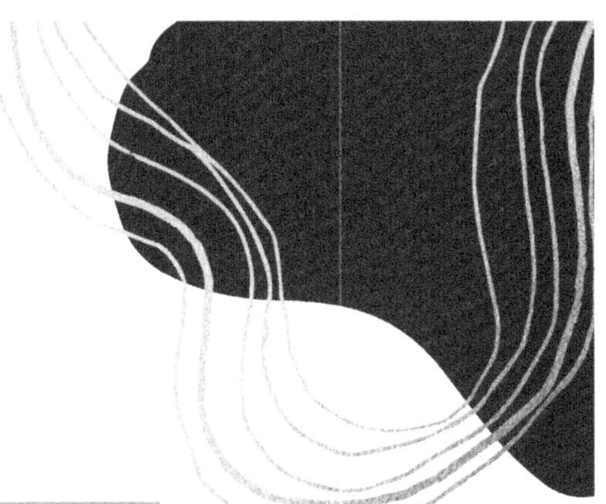

GOALS

- ♡ __________
- ♡ __________
- ♡ __________

TO-DOS

- ♡ __________
- ♡ __________
- ♡ __________

PRAYER POINTS

- ♡ __________
- ♡ __________
- ♡ __________

And the LORD, He is the One who goes before you. He will be with you, He will not leave you nor forsake you; do not fear nor be dismayed.
Deuteronomy 31:8 NKJV

But seek first the kingdom of God and His righteousness,
and all these things shall be added to you.
Matthew 6:33 NKJV

Evening

I will both lie down in peace, and sleep;
For You alone, O Lord, make me dwell in safety.
Palms 4:8 NKJV

WHAT IS GOD SAYING?

Then you will call upon Me and go and pray to Me, and I will listen to you.
Jeremiah 29:12 NKJV

date:________

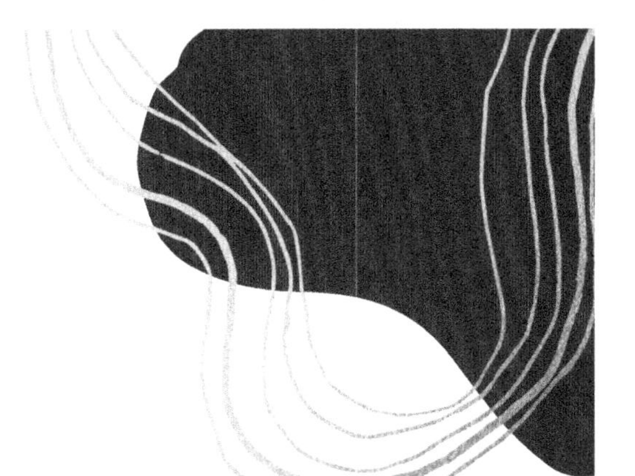

GOALS

♡ ____________________

♡ ____________________

♡ ____________________

TO-DOS

♡ ____________________

♡ ____________________

♡ ____________________

PRAYER POINTS

♡ ____________________

♡ ____________________

♡ ____________________

And the LORD, He is the One who goes before you. He will be with you,
He will not leave you nor forsake you; do not fear nor be dismayed.
Deuteronomy 31:8 NKJV

But seek first the kingdom of God and His righteousness,
and all these things shall be added to you.
Matthew 6:33 NKJV

Evening

I will both lie down in peace, and sleep;
For You alone, O Lord, make me dwell in safety.
Palms 4:8 NKJV

WHAT IS GOD SAYING?

Then you will call upon Me and go and pray to Me, and I will listen to you.
Jeremiah 29:12 NKJV

date: ____________

GOALS

♡ ____________

♡ ____________

♡ ____________

TO-DOS

♡ ____________

♡ ____________

♡ ____________

PRAYER POINTS

♡ ____________

♡ ____________

♡ ____________

And the LORD, He is the One who goes before you. He will be with you, He will not leave you nor forsake you; do not fear nor be dismayed.
Deuteronomy 31:8 NKJV

But seek first the kingdom of God and His righteousness,
and all these things shall be added to you.
Matthew 6:33 NKJV

Evening

I will both lie down in peace, and sleep;
For You alone, O Lord, make me dwell in safety.
Palms 4:8 NKJV

WHAT IS GOD SAYING?

Then you will call upon Me and go and pray to Me, and I will listen to you.
Jeremiah 29:12 NKJV

date: ____________

GOALS

♡ ______________________________

♡ ______________________________

♡ ______________________________

TO-DOS

♡ ______________________________

♡ ______________________________

♡ ______________________________

PRAYER POINTS

♡ ______________________________

♡ ______________________________

♡ ______________________________

And the LORD, He is the One who goes before you. He will be with you,
He will not leave you nor forsake you; do not fear nor be dismayed.
Deuteronomy 31:8 NKJV

But seek first the kingdom of God and His righteousness,
and all these things shall be added to you.
Matthew 6:33 NKJV

Evening

I will both lie down in peace, and sleep;
For You alone, O Lord, make me dwell in safety.
Palms 4:8 NKJV

WHAT IS GOD SAYING?

Then you will call upon Me and go and pray to Me, and I will listen to you.
Jeremiah 29:12 NKJV

date: ____________

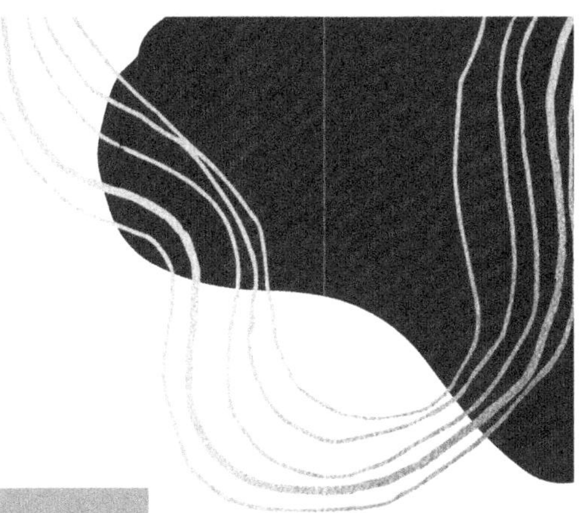

GOALS

♡ ____________________

♡ ____________________

♡ ____________________

TO-DOS

♡ ____________________

♡ ____________________

♡ ____________________

PRAYER POINTS

♡ ____________________

♡ ____________________

♡ ____________________

And the LORD, He is the One who goes before you. He will be with you,
He will not leave you nor forsake you; do not fear nor be dismayed.
Deuteronomy 31:8 NKJV

But seek first the kingdom of God and His righteousness,
and all these things shall be added to you.
Matthew 6:33 NKJV

Evening

I will both lie down in peace, and sleep;
For You alone, O Lord, make me dwell in safety.
Palms 4:8 NKJV

WHAT IS GOD SAYING?

Then you will call upon Me and go and pray to Me, and I will listen to you.
Jeremiah 29:12 NKJV

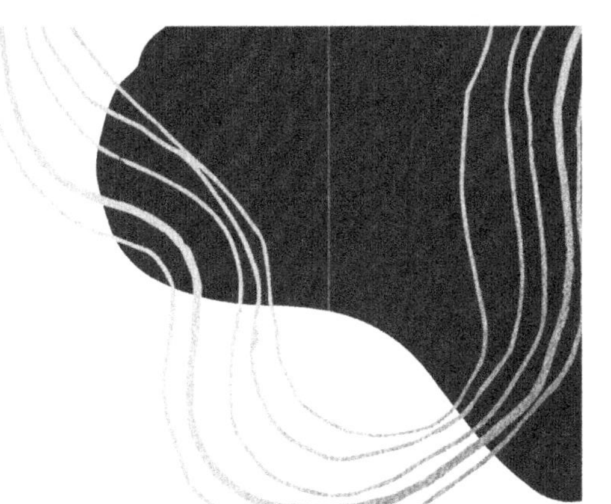

GOALS

♡ ____

♡ ____

♡ ____

TO-DOS

♡ ____

♡ ____

♡ ____

PRAYER POINTS

♡ ____

♡ ____

♡ ____

And the LORD, He is the One who goes before you. He will be with you,
He will not leave you nor forsake you; do not fear nor be dismayed.
Deuteronomy 31:8 NKJV

But seek first the kingdom of God and His righteousness,
and all these things shall be added to you.
Matthew 6:33 NKJV

Evening

I will both lie down in peace, and sleep;
For You alone, O Lord, make me dwell in safety.
Palms 4:8 NKJV

WHAT IS GOD SAYING?

Then you will call upon Me and go and pray to Me, and I will listen to you.
Jeremiah 29:12 NKJV

date: ____________

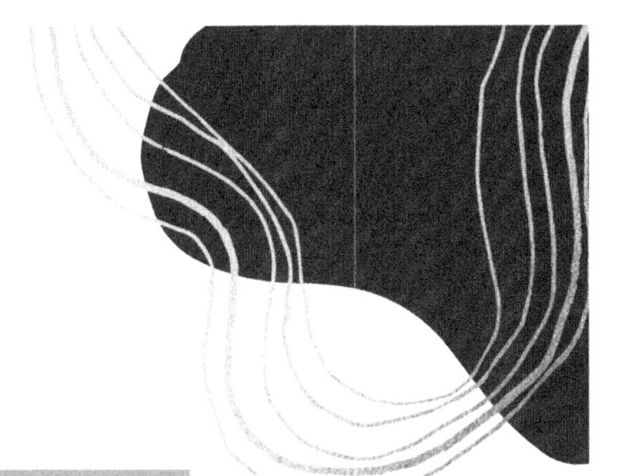

GOALS

♡ ______________________

♡ ______________________

♡ ______________________

TO-DOS

♡ ______________________

♡ ______________________

♡ ______________________

PRAYER POINTS

♡ ______________________

♡ ______________________

♡ ______________________

And the LORD, He is the One who goes before you. He will be with you, He will not leave you nor forsake you; do not fear nor be dismayed.
Deuteronomy 31:8 NKJV

But seek first the kingdom of God and His righteousness,
and all these things shall be added to you.
Matthew 6:33 NKJV

Evening

I will both lie down in peace, and sleep;
For You alone, O Lord, make me dwell in safety.
Palms 4:8 NKJV

WHAT IS GOD SAYING?

Then you will call upon Me and go and pray to Me, and I will listen to you.
Jeremiah 29:12 NKJV

GOALS

♡ ____________________

♡ ____________________

♡ ____________________

TO-DOS

♡ ____________________

♡ ____________________

♡ ____________________

PRAYER POINTS

♡ ____________________

♡ ____________________

♡ ____________________

And the LORD, He is the One who goes before you. He will be with you,
He will not leave you nor forsake you; do not fear nor be dismayed.
Deuteronomy 31:8 NKJV

But seek first the kingdom of God and His righteousness,
and all these things shall be added to you.
Matthew 6:33 NKJV

Evening

I will both lie down in peace, and sleep;
For You alone, O Lord, make me dwell in safety.
Palms 4:8 NKJV

WHAT IS GOD SAYING?

Then you will call upon Me and go and pray to Me, and I will listen to you.
Jeremiah 29:12 NKJV

date:__________

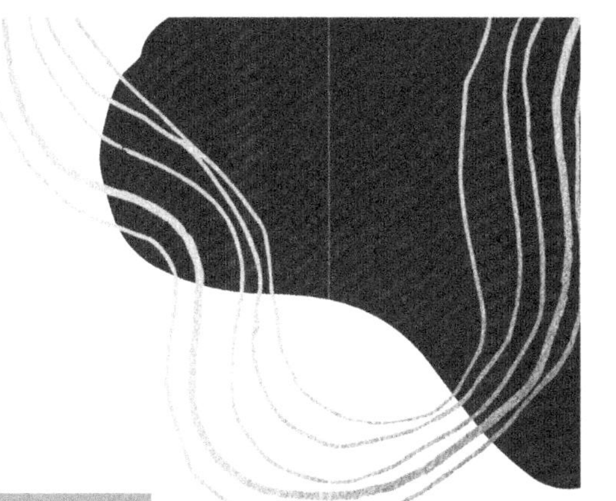

GOALS

♡ ____________________

♡ ____________________

♡ ____________________

TO-DOS

♡ ____________________

♡ ____________________

♡ ____________________

PRAYER POINTS

♡ ____________________

♡ ____________________

♡ ____________________

And the LORD, He is the One who goes before you. He will be with you, He will not leave you nor forsake you; do not fear nor be dismayed.
Deuteronomy 31:8 NKJV

But seek first the kingdom of God and His righteousness,
and all these things shall be added to you.
Matthew 6:33 NKJV

Evening

I will both lie down in peace, and sleep;
For You alone, O Lord, make me dwell in safety.
Palms 4:8 NKJV

WHAT IS GOD SAYING?

Then you will call upon Me and go and pray to Me, and I will listen to you.
Jeremiah 29:12 NKJV

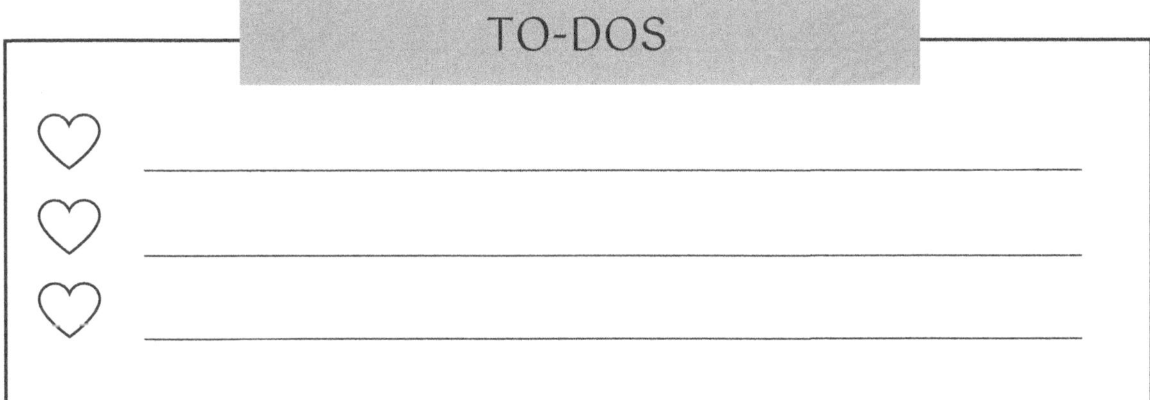

PRAYER POINTS

And the LORD, He is the One who goes before you. He will be with you,
He will not leave you nor forsake you; do not fear nor be dismayed.
Deuteronomy 31:8 NKJV

But seek first the kingdom of God and His righteousness,
and all these things shall be added to you.
Matthew 6:33 NKJV

Evening

I will both lie down in peace, and sleep;
For You alone, O Lord, make me dwell in safety.
Palms 4:8 NKJV

WHAT IS GOD SAYING?

Then you will call upon Me and go and pray to Me, and I will listen to you.
Jeremiah 29:12 NKJV

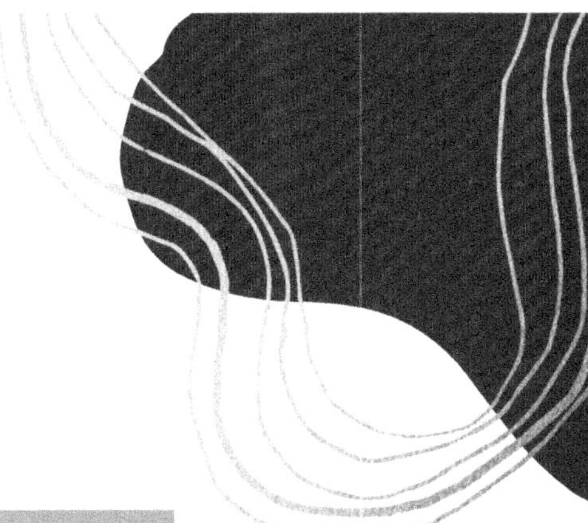

GOALS

♡ ____________________

♡ ____________________

♡ ____________________

TO-DOS

♡ ____________________

♡ ____________________

♡ ____________________

PRAYER POINTS

♡ ____________________

♡ ____________________

♡ ____________________

And the LORD, He is the One who goes before you. He will be with you, He will not leave you nor forsake you; do not fear nor be dismayed.
Deuteronomy 31:8 NKJV

But seek first the kingdom of God and His righteousness,
and all these things shall be added to you.
Matthew 6:33 NKJV

Evening

I will both lie down in peace, and sleep;
For You alone, O Lord, make me dwell in safety.
Palms 4:8 NKJV

WHAT IS GOD SAYING?

Then you will call upon Me and go and pray to Me, and I will listen to you.
Jeremiah 29:12 NKJV

GOALS

♡ ______

♡ ______

♡ ______

TO-DOS

♡ ______

♡ ______

♡ ______

PRAYER POINTS

♡ ______

♡ ______

♡ ______

And the LORD, He is the One who goes before you. He will be with you,
He will not leave you nor forsake you; do not fear nor be dismayed.
Deuteronomy 31:8 NKJV

But seek first the kingdom of God and His righteousness,
and all these things shall be added to you.
Matthew 6:33 NKJV

Evening

I will both lie down in peace, and sleep;
For You alone, O Lord, make me dwell in safety.
Palms 4:8 NKJV

WHAT IS GOD SAYING?

Then you will call upon Me and go and pray to Me, and I will listen to you.
Jeremiah 29:12 NKJV

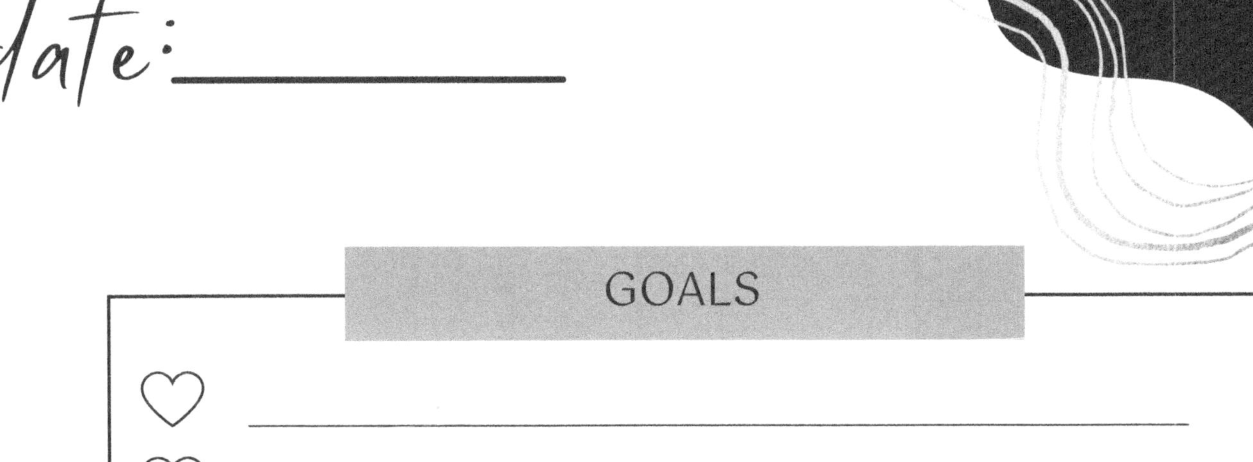

GOALS

TO-DOS

PRAYER POINTS

And the LORD, He is the One who goes before you. He will be with you, He will not leave you nor forsake you; do not fear nor be dismayed.
Deuteronomy 31:8 NKJV

But seek first the kingdom of God and His righteousness,
and all these things shall be added to you.
Matthew 6:33 NKJV

Evening

I will both lie down in peace, and sleep;
For You alone, O Lord, make me dwell in safety.
Palms 4:8 NKJV

WHAT IS GOD SAYING?

Then you will call upon Me and go and pray to Me, and I will listen to you.
Jeremiah 29:12 NKJV

GOALS

TO-DOS

PRAYER POINTS

And the LORD, He is the One who goes before you. He will be with you, He will not leave you nor forsake you; do not fear nor be dismayed.
Deuteronomy 31:8 NKJV

But seek first the kingdom of God and His righteousness,
and all these things shall be added to you.
Matthew 6:33 NKJV

Evening

I will both lie down in peace, and sleep;
For You alone, O Lord, make me dwell in safety.
Palms 4:8 NKJV

WHAT IS GOD SAYING?

Then you will call upon Me and go and pray to Me, and I will listen to you.
Jeremiah 29:12 NKJV

GOALS

♡ ______________________________

♡ ______________________________

♡ ______________________________

TO-DOS

♡ ______________________________

♡ ______________________________

♡ ______________________________

PRAYER POINTS

♡ ______________________________

♡ ______________________________

♡ ______________________________

And the LORD, He is the One who goes before you. He will be with you,
He will not leave you nor forsake you; do not fear nor be dismayed.
Deuteronomy 31:8 NKJV

But seek first the kingdom of God and His righteousness,
and all these things shall be added to you.
Matthew 6:33 NKJV

I will both lie down in peace, and sleep;
For You alone, O Lord, make me dwell in safety.
Palms 4:8 NKJV

WHAT IS GOD SAYING?

Then you will call upon Me and go and pray to Me, and I will listen to you.
Jeremiah 29:12 NKJV

date: ____________

GOALS

- ♡ ____________
- ♡ ____________
- ♡ ____________

TO-DOS

- ♡ ____________
- ♡ ____________
- ♡ ____________

PRAYER POINTS

- ♡ ____________
- ♡ ____________
- ♡ ____________

And the LORD, He is the One who goes before you. He will be with you,
He will not leave you nor forsake you; do not fear nor be dismayed.
Deuteronomy 31:8 NKJV

But seek first the kingdom of God and His righteousness,
and all these things shall be added to you.
Matthew 6:33 NKJV

Evening

I will both lie down in peace, and sleep;
For You alone, O Lord, make me dwell in safety.
Palms 4:8 NKJV

WHAT IS GOD SAYING?

Then you will call upon Me and go and pray to Me, and I will listen to you.
Jeremiah 29:12 NKJV

date:__________

GOALS

♡ ____________________

♡ ____________________

♡ ____________________

TO-DOS

♡ ____________________

♡ ____________________

♡ ____________________

PRAYER POINTS

♡ ____________________

♡ ____________________

♡ ____________________

And the LORD, He is the One who goes before you. He will be with you,
He will not leave you nor forsake you; do not fear nor be dismayed.
Deuteronomy 31:8 NKJV

But seek first the kingdom of God and His righteousness,
and all these things shall be added to you.
Matthew 6:33 NKJV

Evening

I will both lie down in peace, and sleep;
For You alone, O Lord, make me dwell in safety.
Palms 4:8 NKJV

WHAT IS GOD SAYING?

Then you will call upon Me and go and pray to Me, and I will listen to you.
Jeremiah 29:12 NKJV

date: ________

GOALS

♡ ____________________

♡ ____________________

♡ ____________________

TO-DOS

♡ ____________________

♡ ____________________

♡ ____________________

PRAYER POINTS

♡ ____________________

♡ ____________________

♡ ____________________

And the LORD, He is the One who goes before you. He will be with you, He will not leave you nor forsake you; do not fear nor be dismayed.
Deuteronomy 31:8 NKJV

But seek first the kingdom of God and His righteousness,
and all these things shall be added to you.
Matthew 6:33 NKJV

Evening

I will both lie down in peace, and sleep;
For You alone, O Lord, make me dwell in safety.
Palms 4:8 NKJV

WHAT IS GOD SAYING?

Then you will call upon Me and go and pray to Me, and I will listen to you.
Jeremiah 29:12 NKJV

GOALS

♡ ____________________

♡ ____________________

♡ ____________________

TO-DOS

♡ ____________________

♡ ____________________

♡ ____________________

PRAYER POINTS

♡ ____________________

♡ ____________________

♡ ____________________

And the LORD, He is the One who goes before you. He will be with you,
He will not leave you nor forsake you; do not fear nor be dismayed.
Deuteronomy 31:8 NKJV

But seek first the kingdom of God and His righteousness,
and all these things shall be added to you.
Matthew 6:33 NKJV

Evening

I will both lie down in peace, and sleep;
For You alone, O Lord, make me dwell in safety.
Palms 4:8 NKJV

WHAT IS GOD SAYING?

Then you will call upon Me and go and pray to Me, and I will listen to you.
Jeremiah 29:12 NKJV

GOALS

♡ ____________________
♡ ____________________
♡ ____________________

TO-DOS

♡ ____________________
♡ ____________________
♡ ____________________

PRAYER POINTS

♡ ____________________
♡ ____________________
♡ ____________________

And the LORD, He is the One who goes before you. He will be with you,
He will not leave you nor forsake you; do not fear nor be dismayed.
Deuteronomy 31:8 NKJV

But seek first the kingdom of God and His righteousness,
and all these things shall be added to you.
Matthew 6:33 NKJV

Evening

I will both lie down in peace, and sleep;
For You alone, O Lord, make me dwell in safety.
Palms 4:8 NKJV

WHAT IS GOD SAYING?

Then you will call upon Me and go and pray to Me, and I will listen to you.
Jeremiah 29:12 NKJV

GOALS

- ♡ __________
- ♡ __________
- ♡ __________

TO-DOS

- ♡ __________
- ♡ __________
- ♡ __________

PRAYER POINTS

- ♡ __________
- ♡ __________
- ♡ __________

And the LORD, He is the One who goes before you. He will be with you,
He will not leave you nor forsake you; do not fear nor be dismayed.
Deuteronomy 31:8 NKJV

But seek first the kingdom of God and His righteousness,
and all these things shall be added to you.
Matthew 6:33 NKJV

Evening

I will both lie down in peace, and sleep;
For You alone, O Lord, make me dwell in safety.
Palms 4:8 NKJV

WHAT IS GOD SAYING?

Then you will call upon Me and go and pray to Me, and I will listen to you.
Jeremiah 29:12 NKJV

GOALS

TO-DOS

PRAYER POINTS

And the LORD, He is the One who goes before you. He will be with you,
He will not leave you nor forsake you; do not fear nor be dismayed.
Deuteronomy 31:8 NKJV

But seek first the kingdom of God and His righteousness,
and all these things shall be added to you.
Matthew 6:33 NKJV

Evening

I will both lie down in peace, and sleep;
For You alone, O Lord, make me dwell in safety.
Palms 4:8 NKJV

WHAT IS GOD SAYING?

Then you will call upon Me and go and pray to Me, and I will listen to you.
Jeremiah 29:12 NKJV

GOALS

♡ ____________________

♡ ____________________

♡ ____________________

TO-DOS

♡ ____________________

♡ ____________________

♡ ____________________

PRAYER POINTS

♡ ____________________

♡ ____________________

♡ ____________________

And the LORD, He is the One who goes before you. He will be with you,
He will not leave you nor forsake you; do not fear nor be dismayed.
Deuteronomy 31:8 NKJV

But seek first the kingdom of God and His righteousness,
and all these things shall be added to you.
Matthew 6:33 NKJV

Evening

I will both lie down in peace, and sleep;
For You alone, O Lord, make me dwell in safety.
Palms 4:8 NKJV

WHAT IS GOD SAYING?

Then you will call upon Me and go and pray to Me, and I will listen to you.
Jeremiah 29:12 NKJV

date:

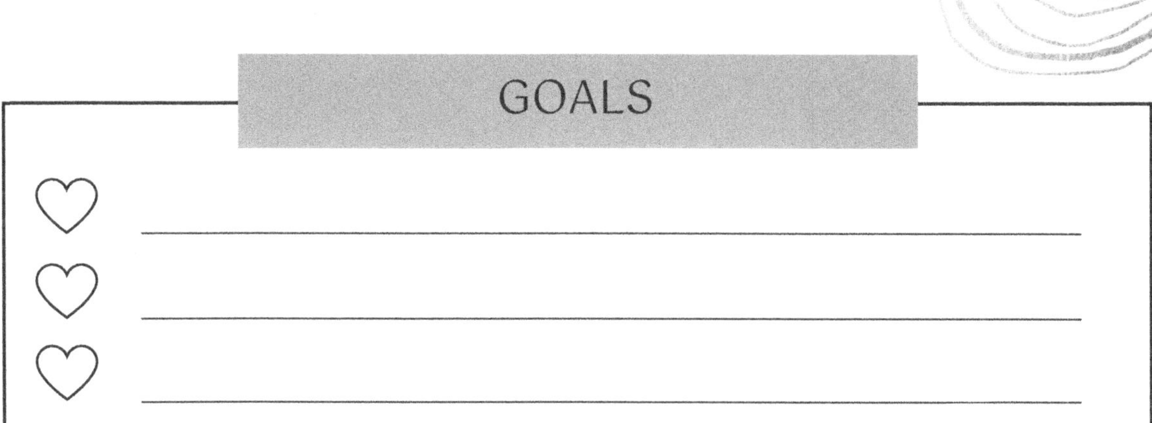

GOALS

♡ ____

♡ ____

♡ ____

TO-DOS

♡ ____

♡ ____

♡ ____

PRAYER POINTS

♡ ____

♡ ____

♡ ____

And the LORD, He is the One who goes before you. He will be with you,
He will not leave you nor forsake you; do not fear nor be dismayed.
Deuteronomy 31:8 NKJV

But seek first the kingdom of God and His righteousness,
and all these things shall be added to you.
Matthew 6:33 NKJV

I will both lie down in peace, and sleep;
For You alone, O Lord, make me dwell in safety.
Palms 4:8 NKJV

WHAT IS GOD SAYING?

Then you will call upon Me and go and pray to Me, and I will listen to you.
Jeremiah 29:12 NKJV

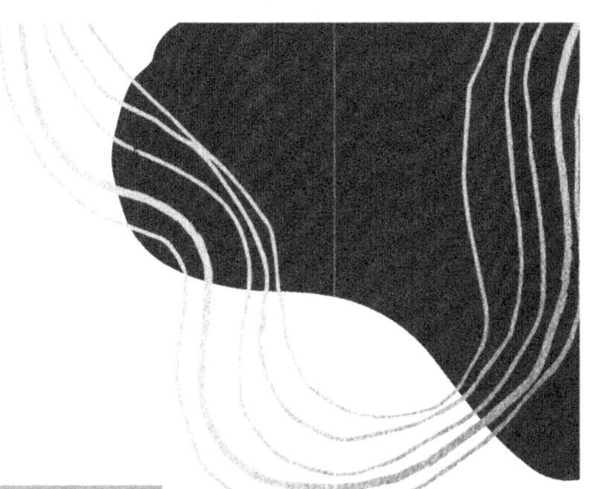

GOALS

♡ ____________________

♡ ____________________

♡ ____________________

TO-DOS

♡ ____________________

♡ ____________________

♡ ____________________

PRAYER POINTS

♡ ____________________

♡ ____________________

♡ ____________________

And the LORD, He is the One who goes before you. He will be with you,
He will not leave you nor forsake you; do not fear nor be dismayed.
Deuteronomy 31:8 NKJV

But seek first the kingdom of God and His righteousness,
and all these things shall be added to you.
Matthew 6:33 NKJV

Evening

I will both lie down in peace, and sleep;
For You alone, O Lord, make me dwell in safety.
Palms 4:8 NKJV

WHAT IS GOD SAYING?

Then you will call upon Me and go and pray to Me, and I will listen to you.
Jeremiah 29:12 NKJV

date:

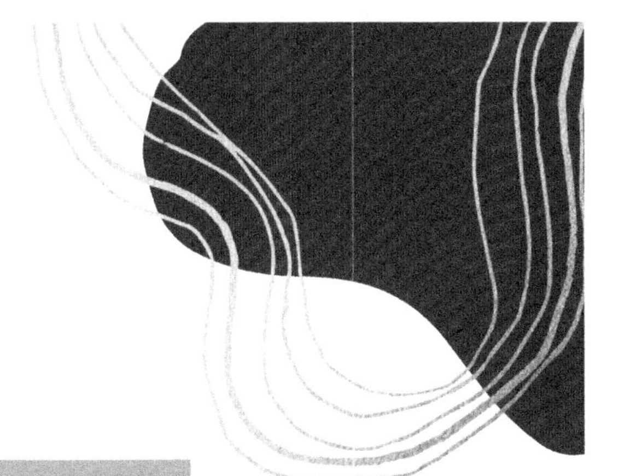

GOALS

TO-DOS

PRAYER POINTS

And the LORD, He is the One who goes before you. He will be with you, He will not leave you nor forsake you; do not fear nor be dismayed.

Deuteronomy 31:8 NKJV

But seek first the kingdom of God and His righteousness,
and all these things shall be added to you.
Matthew 6:33 NKJV

Evening

I will both lie down in peace, and sleep;
For You alone, O Lord, make me dwell in safety.
Palms 4:8 NKJV

WHAT IS GOD SAYING?

Then you will call upon Me and go and pray to Me, and I will listen to you.
Jeremiah 29:12 NKJV

date: ____________

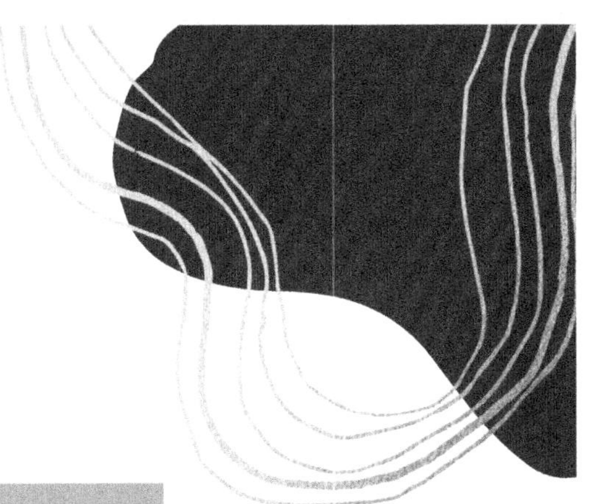

GOALS

♡ ____________

♡ ____________

♡ ____________

TO-DOS

♡ ____________

♡ ____________

♡ ____________

PRAYER POINTS

♡ ____________

♡ ____________

♡ ____________

And the LORD, He is the One who goes before you. He will be with you,
He will not leave you nor forsake you; do not fear nor be dismayed.
Deuteronomy 31:8 NKJV

But seek first the kingdom of God and His righteousness,
and all these things shall be added to you.
Matthew 6:33 NKJV

Evening

I will both lie down in peace, and sleep;
For You alone, O Lord, make me dwell in safety.
Palms 4:8 NKJV

WHAT IS GOD SAYING?

Then you will call upon Me and go and pray to Me, and I will listen to you.
Jeremiah 29:12 NKJV

date:________

GOALS

♡ ________

♡ ________

♡ ________

TO-DOS

♡ ________

♡ ________

♡ ________

PRAYER POINTS

♡ ________

♡ ________

♡ ________

And the LORD, He is the One who goes before you. He will be with you,
He will not leave you nor forsake you; do not fear nor be dismayed.
Deuteronomy 31:8 NKJV

But seek first the kingdom of God and His righteousness,
and all these things shall be added to you.
Matthew 6:33 NKJV

Evening

I will both lie down in peace, and sleep;
For You alone, O Lord, make me dwell in safety.
Palms 4:8 NKJV

WHAT IS GOD SAYING?

Then you will call upon Me and go and pray to Me, and I will listen to you.
Jeremiah 29:12 NKJV

date:

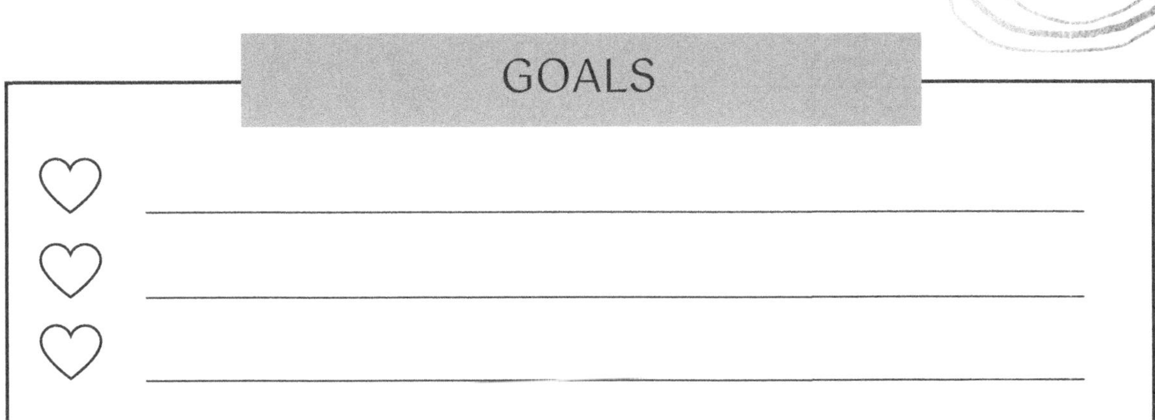

TO-DOS

PRAYER POINTS

And the LORD, He is the One who goes before you. He will be with you, He will not leave you nor forsake you; do not fear nor be dismayed.
Deuteronomy 31:8 NKJV

But seek first the kingdom of God and His righteousness,
and all these things shall be added to you.
Matthew 6:33 NKJV

Evening

I will both lie down in peace, and sleep;
For You alone, O Lord, make me dwell in safety.
Palms 4:8 NKJV

WHAT IS GOD SAYING?

Then you will call upon Me and go and pray to Me, and I will listen to you.
Jeremiah 29:12 NKJV

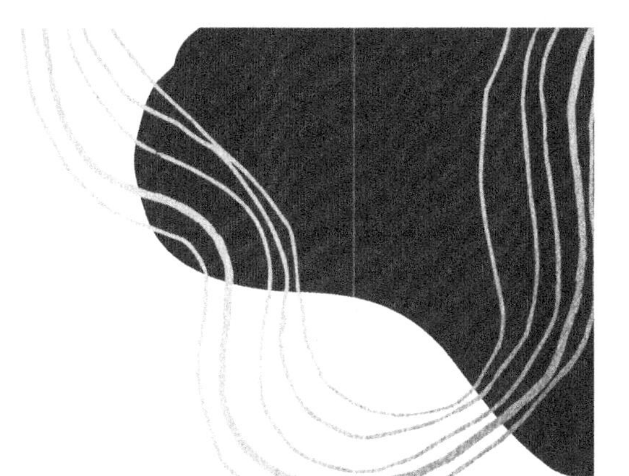

GOALS

TO-DOS

PRAYER POINTS

And the LORD, He is the One who goes before you. He will be with you, He will not leave you nor forsake you; do not fear nor be dismayed.
Deuteronomy 31:8 NKJV

But seek first the kingdom of God and His righteousness,
and all these things shall be added to you.
Matthew 6:33 NKJV

Evening

I will both lie down in peace, and sleep;
For You alone, O Lord, make me dwell in safety.
Palms 4:8 NKJV

WHAT IS GOD SAYING?

Then you will call upon Me and go and pray to Me, and I will listen to you.
Jeremiah 29:12 NKJV

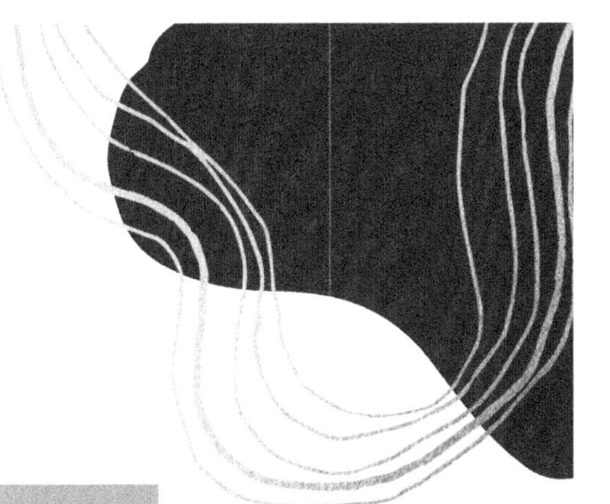

GOALS

♡ ____________________

♡ ____________________

♡ ____________________

TO-DOS

♡ ____________________

♡ ____________________

♡ ____________________

PRAYER POINTS

♡ ____________________

♡ ____________________

♡ ____________________

And the LORD, He is the One who goes before you. He will be with you,
He will not leave you nor forsake you; do not fear nor be dismayed.
Deuteronomy 31:8 NKJV

But seek first the kingdom of God and His righteousness,
and all these things shall be added to you.
Matthew 6:33 NKJV

Evening

I will both lie down in peace, and sleep;
For You alone, O Lord, make me dwell in safety.
Palms 4:8 NKJV

WHAT IS GOD SAYING?

Then you will call upon Me and go and pray to Me, and I will listen to you.
Jeremiah 29:12 NKJV

GOALS

♡ ______________________
♡ ______________________
♡ ______________________

TO-DOS

♡ ______________________
♡ ______________________
♡ ______________________

PRAYER POINTS

♡ ______________________
♡ ______________________
♡ ______________________

And the LORD, He is the One who goes before you. He will be with you, He will not leave you nor forsake you; do not fear nor be dismayed.
Deuteronomy 31:8 NKJV

But seek first the kingdom of God and His righteousness,
and all these things shall be added to you.
Matthew 6:33 NKJV

Evening

I will both lie down in peace, and sleep;
For You alone, O Lord, make me dwell in safety.
Palms 4:8 NKJV

WHAT IS GOD SAYING?

Then you will call upon Me and go and pray to Me, and I will listen to you.
Jeremiah 29:12 NKJV

date: ____________

GOALS

♡ ____________

♡ ____________

♡ ____________

TO-DOS

♡ ____________

♡ ____________

♡ ____________

PRAYER POINTS

♡ ____________

♡ ____________

♡ ____________

And the LORD, He is the One who goes before you. He will be with you, He will not leave you nor forsake you; do not fear nor be dismayed.
Deuteronomy 31:8 NKJV

But seek first the kingdom of God and His righteousness,
and all these things shall be added to you.
Matthew 6:33 NKJV

Evening

I will both lie down in peace, and sleep;
For You alone, O Lord, make me dwell in safety.
Palms 4:8 NKJV

WHAT IS GOD SAYING?

Then you will call upon Me and go and pray to Me, and I will listen to you.
Jeremiah 29:12 NKJV

date:

GOALS

TO-DOS

PRAYER POINTS

And the LORD, He is the One who goes before you. He will be with you, He will not leave you nor forsake you; do not fear nor be dismayed.
Deuteronomy 31:8 NKJV

But seek first the kingdom of God and His righteousness,
and all these things shall be added to you.
Matthew 6:33 NKJV

Evening

I will both lie down in peace, and sleep;
For You alone, O Lord, make me dwell in safety.
Palms 4:8 NKJV

WHAT IS GOD SAYING?

Then you will call upon Me and go and pray to Me, and I will listen to you.
Jeremiah 29:12 NKJV

date: ____________

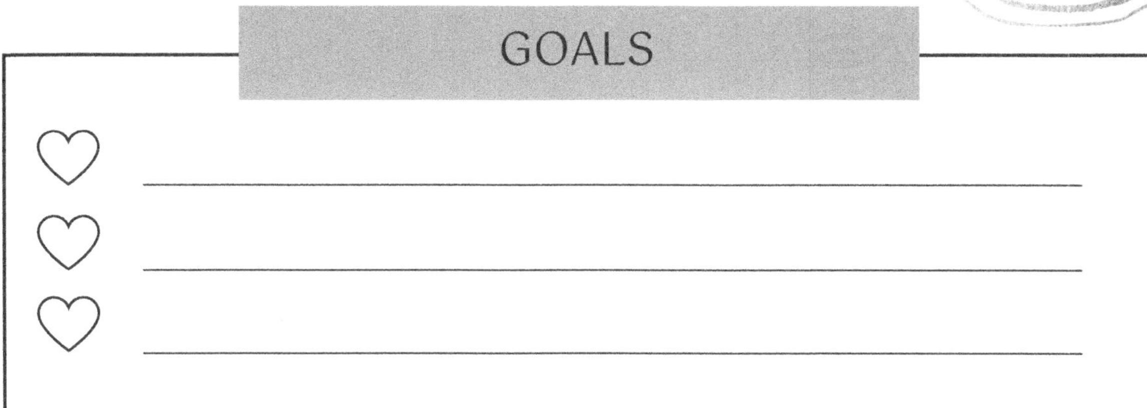

TO-DOS

PRAYER POINTS

And the LORD, He is the One who goes before you. He will be with you,
He will not leave you nor forsake you; do not fear nor be dismayed.
Deuteronomy 31:8 NKJV

But seek first the kingdom of God and His righteousness,
and all these things shall be added to you.
Matthew 6:33 NKJV

Evening

I will both lie down in peace, and sleep;
For You alone, O Lord, make me dwell in safety.
Palms 4:8 NKJV

WHAT IS GOD SAYING?

Then you will call upon Me and go and pray to Me, and I will listen to you.
Jeremiah 29:12 NKJV

date:__________

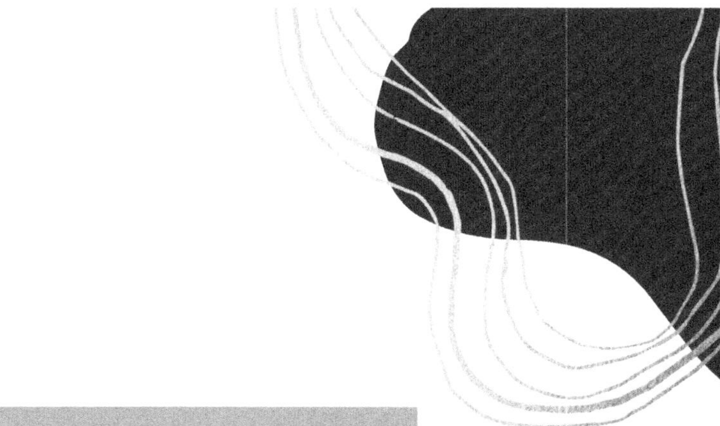

GOALS

♡ ____________________

♡ ____________________

♡ ____________________

TO-DOS

♡ ____________________

♡ ____________________

♡ ____________________

PRAYER POINTS

♡ ____________________

♡ ____________________

♡ ____________________

And the LORD, He is the One who goes before you. He will be with you,
He will not leave you nor forsake you; do not fear nor be dismayed.
Deuteronomy 31:8 NKJV

But seek first the kingdom of God and His righteousness,
and all these things shall be added to you.
Matthew 6:33 NKJV

Evening

I will both lie down in peace, and sleep;
For You alone, O Lord, make me dwell in safety.
Palms 4:8 NKJV

WHAT IS GOD SAYING?

Then you will call upon Me and go and pray to Me, and I will listen to you.
Jeremiah 29:12 NKJV

date: ____________

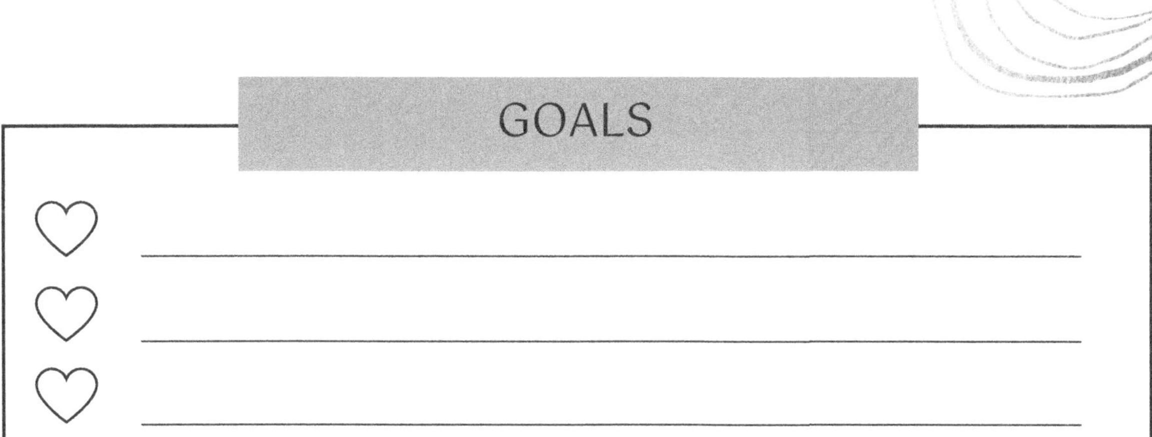

GOALS

- ♡ ____________
- ♡ ____________
- ♡ ____________

TO-DOS

- ♡ ____________
- ♡ ____________
- ♡ ____________

PRAYER POINTS

- ♡ ____________
- ♡ ____________
- ♡ ____________

And the LORD, He is the One who goes before you. He will be with you,
He will not leave you nor forsake you; do not fear nor be dismayed.
Deuteronomy 31:8 NKJV

But seek first the kingdom of God and His righteousness,
and all these things shall be added to you.
Matthew 6:33 NKJV

Evening

I will both lie down in peace, and sleep;
For You alone, O Lord, make me dwell in safety.
Palms 4:8 NKJV

WHAT IS GOD SAYING?

Then you will call upon Me and go and pray to Me, and I will listen to you.
Jeremiah 29:12 NKJV

date: ____________

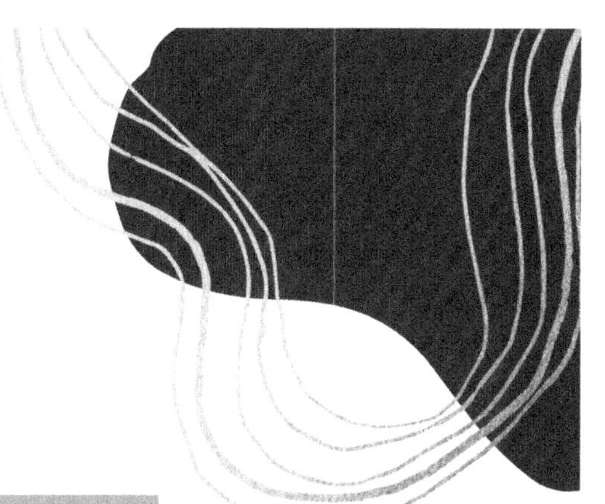

GOALS

♡ ____________________
♡ ____________________
♡ ____________________

TO-DOS

♡ ____________________
♡ ____________________
♡ ____________________

PRAYER POINTS

♡ ____________________
♡ ____________________
♡ ____________________

And the LORD, He is the One who goes before you. He will be with you, He will not leave you nor forsake you; do not fear nor be dismayed.
Deuteronomy 31:8 NKJV

But seek first the kingdom of God and His righteousness,
and all these things shall be added to you.
Matthew 6:33 NKJV

Evening

I will both lie down in peace, and sleep;
For You alone, O Lord, make me dwell in safety.
Palms 4:8 NKJV

WHAT IS GOD SAYING?

Then you will call upon Me and go and pray to Me, and I will listen to you.
Jeremiah 29:12 NKJV

GOALS

- ♡ ______
- ♡ ______
- ♡ ______

TO-DOS

- ♡ ______
- ♡ ______
- ♡ ______

PRAYER POINTS

- ♡ ______
- ♡ ______
- ♡ ______

And the LORD, He is the One who goes before you. He will be with you,
He will not leave you nor forsake you; do not fear nor be dismayed.
Deuteronomy 31:8 NKJV

But seek first the kingdom of God and His righteousness,
and all these things shall be added to you.
Matthew 6:33 NKJV

Evening

I will both lie down in peace, and sleep;
For You alone, O Lord, make me dwell in safety.
Palms 4:8 NKJV

WHAT IS GOD SAYING?

Then you will call upon Me and go and pray to Me, and I will listen to you.
Jeremiah 29:12 NKJV

GOALS

♡ ______

♡ ______

♡ ______

TO-DOS

♡ ______

♡ ______

♡ ______

PRAYER POINTS

♡ ______

♡ ______

♡ ______

And the LORD, He is the One who goes before you. He will be with you,
He will not leave you nor forsake you; do not fear nor be dismayed.
Deuteronomy 31:8 NKJV

But seek first the kingdom of God and His righteousness,
and all these things shall be added to you.
Matthew 6:33 NKJV

Evening

I will both lie down in peace, and sleep;
For You alone, O Lord, make me dwell in safety.
Palms 4:8 NKJV

WHAT IS GOD SAYING?

Then you will call upon Me and go and pray to Me, and I will listen to you.
Jeremiah 29:12 NKJV

date:

GOALS

TO-DOS

PRAYER POINTS

And the LORD, He is the One who goes before you. He will be with you, He will not leave you nor forsake you; do not fear nor be dismayed.
Deuteronomy 31:8 NKJV

But seek first the kingdom of God and His righteousness,
and all these things shall be added to you.
Matthew 6:33 NKJV

Evening

I will both lie down in peace, and sleep;
For You alone, O Lord, make me dwell in safety.
Palms 4:8 NKJV

WHAT IS GOD SAYING?

Then you will call upon Me and go and pray to Me, and I will listen to you.
Jeremiah 29:12 NKJV

Made in the USA
Coppell, TX
25 April 2024